Discovering
Cultures

Italy

Margaret Gay Malone

BENCHMARK BOOKS

MARSHALL CAVENDISH
NEW YORK

For my grandnieces, Lauren Mahon and Morgan and Kristen Tursi, and my grandnephew, Ryan Mahon—MGM

With thanks to Dennis Looney, Chair, Department of French and Italian, University of Pittsburgh,
for the careful review of this manuscript.

Acknowledgments

My thanks to Paola LoPiccolo and her relatives in Italy. Her sister, Roberta Provoli Stoppa, and her nine-year-old niece, Giulia Stoppa, generously shared their time and expertise about their country. Thanks too, to Dr. Bill LiPara, for his recollections of his Italian childhood. And to Ida Donaggio Sturge, a most knowledgeable teacher of Italian, her native tongue.

Benchmark Books
Marshall Cavendish
99 White Plains Road, Tarrytown, New York 10591-9001
Text copyright © 2003 by Marshall Cavendish Corporation
Map and illustrations copyright © 2003 by Marshall Cavendish Corporation
Map and illustrations by Salvatore Murdocca
Book design by Virginia Pope
All rights reserved. No part of this book may be reproduced in any form without written permission from the publisher.

Library of Congress Cataloging-in-Publication Data

Malone, Margaret Gay.
Italy / by Margaret Gay Malone.
p. cm. — (Discovering cultures)
Includes bibliographical references and index.
Summary: Highlights the geography, people, food, schools, recreation, celebrations, and language of Italy.
ISBN 0-7614-1176-3
1. Italy—Juvenile literature. [1.Italy.] I. Title. II. Series.
DG417 .M28 2003
945—dc21   2001007458

Photo Research by Candlepants Incorporated
Cover Photo: Corbis/ Hugh Rooney; Eye Ubiquitous

The photographs in this book are used by permission and through the courtesy of; Corbis: Bob Krist, 1; John Hesletine, 6; Paul Almasy, 8; Paul Thompson/Ecoscene, 9; Dennis Degnan, 10 (left); Bettmann, 10 (right), 15, 44 (left & right); Roger Ressmeyer, 11; Owen Franken, 12, 23, 24, 32, 33; Hubert Stadler, 13, 40; John & Dallas Heaton, 14; Peter Harholdt, 16-17; David Turnley, 18; Michael T. Sedam, 20; James Marshall, 21; Michael S. Yamashita, 26; Annie Griffiths Belt, 27; Richard Hamilton Smith, 30; Karl Weatherly, 31 (left), Ales Fevzer, 31 (right); AFP, 36, 37; Danial Laine, 38; Yann-Arthus Bertrand, 39; ReutersNewMedia, 45; Tim Gipstein, back cover. Getty Images: Stone/Louis Grandam, 4-5; The Image Bank/Mario Carbone, 22. Mercury Press.com ©2002: Vision/Remo di Adamo, 19; Vision/Mauro Sorani, 35; Alberto Cagliano, 41. Bruce Coleman Inc.: Donadani, 29; Charles Henneghein, 34.

Cover: *The Colosseum of Rome*; Title page: *A masked woman during Carnevale in Venice*

Printed in Hong Kong

1 3 5 6 4 2

Turn the Pages...

Buon giorno! Ciao!

(Good day! Hello!)

Welcome to Italy!

In the shadow of Saint Peter's Basilica in Rome, a boy stops for a drink.

Where in the World Is Italy?

Italy is a country in western Europe. It is easy to spot on a map. The country looks like a boot in the Mediterranean Sea. At the toe is the island of Sicily and to the west lies the island of Sardinia.

Italy is more than six hundred miles (966 kilometers) long. That's about a hundred miles longer than Florida. Also like Florida, more than half of Italy is a peninsula, with water on three sides. Italians enjoy pleasant summers and snowy winters in the north. In the south, the winters are mild, and the summers are hot and dry. The climate in north central Italy is right for growing grapes for wine and in the south for growing olives, which are made into olive oil. Italian olive oil and wines are sold to many other countries.

Olive trees on an Italian hillside

Mont Blanc

Milan

Po

Venice

Florence

Adriatic Sea

★ Rome

Naples

Pompeii

Sardinia

Mediterranean Sea

Sicily

Mount Etna

N
NW   NE
W   E
SW   SE
S

The Dolomites are a major mountain range in northern Italy.

Mountains cover much of Italy. At the top of the boot are the Alps and the Dolomites. They border France, Switzerland, Austria, and Slovenia. Italy shares its highest mountain, Mont Blanc, with France and Switzerland. Running the length of the boot are the Apennines.

Some Italians live at the base of volcanoes like Mount Vesuvius and Mount Etna, the highest active volcano in Europe. When these volcanoes erupt, they spill hot lava across the nearby countryside. Scientists study the volcanoes to warn people to leave before an eruption. But when Mount Etna is dormant, which is most of the time, it is a good place to ski. There are cries of *Attenzione!* (Look out!) as skiers fly down the slopes.

Italy has thousands of miles of coastline. Many Italians live near the coast in port cities, such as Naples. But the sea is not the only body of water. Four lakes at the bottom of the Alps were formed thousands of years ago by melting glaciers. The banks of the Po, Italy's longest river, have rich land for farming rice and other crops.

Mount Etna rises through the snow.

Pope John Paul II blesses the crowd in Saint Peter's Square.

A gondola glides through a Venetian canal.

Rome is Italy's capital and largest city. Inside Rome is Vatican City, the center of the Catholic Church and the home of its leader, the pope. The Vatican is often called "a city within a city" because it has its own government. Venice, in the north, may be the most unusual city in the world. It is built on a group of low-lying islands in the Adriatic Sea. The city's "streets" are canals. Venetians get around by boat or by walking over the city's many beautiful bridges.

Pompeii

Pompeii was an ancient city, bustling with thousands of people. The citizens of Pompeii could look up and see Mount Vesuvius, a volcano that rose above their homes. Centuries ago, it did not look like a volcano, much less an active one. It was quiet and covered with a forest where wild boars lived. Then, in A.D. 79, it erupted, hurling burning ash and stones on the city below. The eruption caught the people by surprise. Most of them fled, but about two thousand stayed and were killed. Thirteen feet of wet ash preserved their bodies as they went about their business—eating, working, and sleeping. Mount Vesuvius has erupted several times since that fateful day thousands of years ago. It was not until the eighteenth century that people discovered the buried city of Pompeii. Now it is a place where archaeologists and tourists learn more about life in the past.

What Makes Italy Italian?

Italians enjoy life. Almost any day is a reason to celebrate. In fact, no other country in Europe celebrates as often. Lively music, colorful festivals, and shouts of *Mangia!* (Eat!) as family and friends sit down for a meal are what makes Italy Italian.

Ask Italians what is most important to them, and they will say family. In the past, grandparents, aunts, uncles, and cousins all lived together. Today, parents and their children share an apartment. Sometimes grandparents live with them, too. Extended families still get together often. They greet each other with hugs and kisses. The restaurants where they meet for meals come alive with their chatter and laughter.

*Men meet in the street to
chat, a favorite pastime.*

Italian children are much loved. Parents and grandparents have affectionate names for them. They call them *tesoro* (treasure), *stella d'oro* (golden star), or *gioia* (joy). On farms in the south, children are given many chores, but city children often have only a few chores, such as cleaning their room and setting the table. Because doing well in school is most important, they usually do not have after-school jobs.

Italians are social people. They love to talk—and argue—in cafés, at the market, and on the street corner. They are famous for speaking with their hands. They wave their hands around in gestures that show anger, surprise, and joy.

Michelangelo's Pietà is one of Italy's treasures.

Italy is known for its fine art and architecture. Artisans create beautiful crafts such as colorful Venetian glass, soft leather, and lace. The buildings of Florence and Venice are rich with carvings. The Colosseum in Rome is a large outdoor theater that has lasted almost two thousand years. And the paintings and sculpture of Italian artists, from the ancient Romans to the Renaissance artist Michelangelo, are still admired in museums today.

Italians know how to make music and musical instruments. On the rooftops of Cremona, violins hang on lines like laundry! These beautiful instruments are made of many different kinds of wood. The violin makers apply layers of varnish until each violin glows. The finished instrument is a work of art.

The Duomo, also called the Cathedral of Milan, is an example of fine Italian architecture.

In the United States, many things we enjoy come from Italy. More than four hundred years ago, opera was born in the city of Florence. American children know the story of Pinocchio, which was written in Italy more than a hundred years ago. Many people prize the quality of Italian sports cars and Italian shoes and handbags. And it seems everyone in America loves a slice of pizza! Pizza and pasta come from Italy, too.

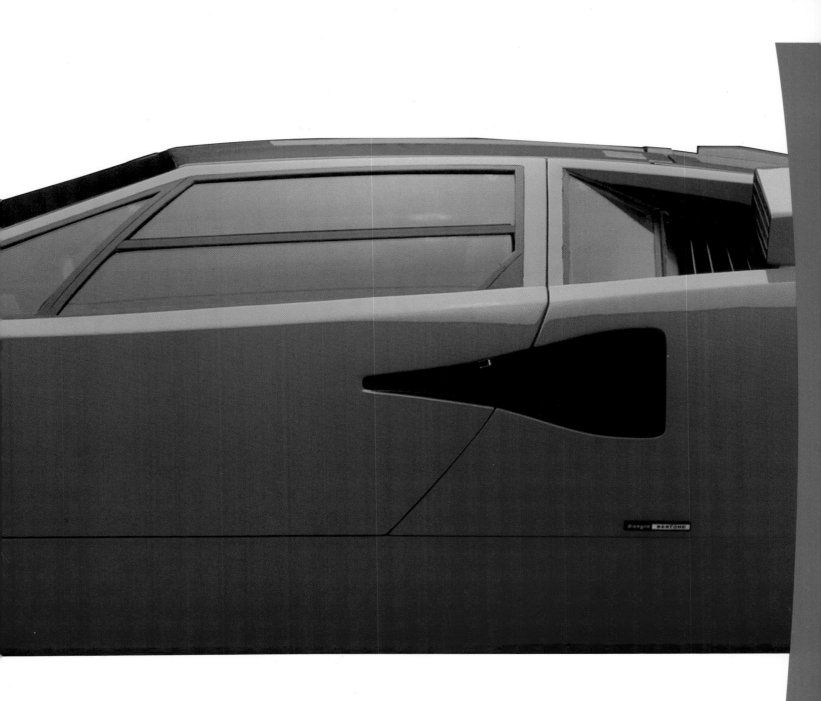

Italy manufactures sports cars like this Lamborghini.

Music makes the marketplace lively.

Many Americans travel to Italy. They bring American culture with them. Young Italians wear jeans and enjoy American music. Italian children love to watch Topolino and Paperino in the movies. Americans know them as Mickey Mouse and Donald Duck. After watching an American movie, children in Italy's big cities can go to McDonald's for a *hamburgher* (hamburger), *patatine* (fries), and a Coke.

Do you speak Italian? You may not know it, but when you use words such as piano, studio, spaghetti, ravioli, and salami, you are speaking Italian. These words are clues to things Italians love—music, art, and food!

Venetian Glass

Venetian glass is known for its rich colors and tiny flowerlike designs. Like many of Italy's traditions, the art of making Venetian glass dates back thousands of years. Glass masters use the same glass-blowing pipes, instruments, and furnaces that have been used throughout the ages. It takes time and expertise to create the delicate glass vases, sculptures, chandeliers, and jewelry. First liquid glass is heated to about 932 degrees Fahrenheit (500 degrees Celsius). Then before it cools and becomes solid, the glass master blows or stretches it to just the right shape.

Living in Italy

Italy is one of the most crowded countries in Europe. Before World War II, half the country lived on farms or in villages. After the war, people moved to the cities. Now, almost 75 percent live in cities and towns.

People like to throw coins into Rome's Trevi Fountain.

Italian cities look different from American cities. The city of Florence is a thousand years old. Rome is two thousand! Public buildings and churches are trimmed with carvings, columns, and statues. In villages, homes are close together and the streets are narrow and paved with cobblestones. Every village has a *piazza* (town square) where people gather, usually with a decorative fountain and carved statues in the center.

Most city people live in apartments. They usually have a living-dining room, a kitchen, two bedrooms, and a bath. Many of the buildings are old, with beautiful architectural details. Newer apartments dot the suburbs. Because Italians like to garden, their balconies are often overflowing with colorful plants. Some villages hold contests to judge the prettiest balcony garden.

Italians decorate their balconies with plants and flowers.

Country children live in farmhouses. If they keep farm animals, like chickens or pigs, the children's chore is to feed them. Italian farmers grow many kinds of fruits and vegetables, wheat, soybeans, sunflowers, and grapes for wine. Italian wines are some of the most famous in the world.

There are very few shopping malls and department stores in Italy. Children and their parents buy clothes in small shops. In the villages and in the cities, Italians like the personal attention they get there. They also enjoy bargaining for lower prices with vendors at outdoor markets. There they can find a variety of fresh foods. Italians spend more money on food than the people of many other nations.

Country children help care for farm animals.

Italy is the home of pasta.

Most Italians start their day with a light meal of crusty bread and jam. Grownups drink strong coffee with it, while children drink warm milk. It is served in a bowl, good for dunking! Except in the biggest northern cities, lunches are large, and dinners are, too.

Italians serve pasta for lunch and dinner. Most pasta is topped with tomato sauce. Tomatoes came to Italy from Mexico about five hundred years ago. At first, people thought the tomato plant was poisonous. Some brave person finally cooked the tomatoes and discovered a sauce for pasta. Italians have been enjoying it ever since.

The main meal, lunch, begins with antipasto, an

appetizer of cold meats. In the north, where rice is grown, *risotto* replaces pasta. Bread on the table is a must. Italians buy crusty loaves of bread fresh every day. They do not spread butter on it, but they may dip it in sauce or olive oil. Meat or fish, vegetables, wine, and dessert—usually fruit—complete the meal. And ice cream, called *gelato*, is a favorite any time!

A girl enjoys gelato, *Italian ice cream.*

Let's Eat!
Baked Ziti

Ziti is just one of the many kinds of pasta. Ziti are little tubes, much shorter and fatter than spaghetti. They can be boiled and covered with tomato sauce or olive oil and garlic, but they are often baked. Ask an adult to help you prepare this recipe.

Ingredients:

1 pound ziti

1 cup ricotta cheese

2 eight-ounce cans tomato sauce

6 ounces mozzarella, diced

Salt and pepper to taste

4 ounces mozzarella, thinly sliced

1/4 cup grated parmesan cheese

Wash your hands. Preheat oven to 350 degrees. Cook ziti as directed on the package. Drain. Combine ricotta and tomato sauce. Pour over ziti and mix. Add diced mozzarella. Add salt and pepper if you wish. Mix. Place in a two-quart casserole. Cover with sliced mozzarella. Sprinkle with parmesan cheese. Bake fifteen minutes, uncovered, until it is lightly browned.
Serves six.

School Days

On any school day, boys and girls can be seen walking or bicycling to school. Others get a ride with their parents. Yellow school buses take a few children to school. Public school students dress casually in jeans, sweaters, and sweatshirts. But children who attend private schools wear uniforms.

In central Italy, children go to school from early September to June. In the south, where the summer is long and hot, school starts at the end of September. Parents can send their children to school for half a day or a whole day. Most children go to school half a day, from 8:15 A.M. to 12:30 P.M. Two days a week, these half-day students go back in the afternoon. Some

Boys in uniform walk to school.

Children go to school six days a week.

working parents send their children to school for the whole day from 8:30 A.M. until 4:15 P.M.

Work stops for fifteen minutes every morning for a quick snack of fruit or a sandwich. But lunch is almost two hours long, and school lunches are big. In the cafeteria, the children do not get their own food. They sit at tables and are served by the school's lunch staff. Children start with pasta with tomato sauce, soup, or gnocchi, a type of dumpling. Then they have a hot main course. This might be meat, chicken, fish, cheese, or eggs. A salad and cooked vegetables complete the main course. For dessert, children eat fruit or yogurt.

Italian children are serious about school. They go six days a week. Sunday is their only day off. In primary school, which lasts five years, students learn reading and writing. They begin to study another language in first grade. Most children learn English, but some study German or French. Students study math

27

Children study science in an elementary school.

and science, social studies, art, and music. They participate in gym class. Because Italy is a Catholic country, children also study the Catholic religion.

Children have to go to school only from age six to fourteen, but most study longer. Middle school begins at age eleven and lasts three years. Secondary school is five years. If students pass their exams, they get a diploma and can go on to a university.

Many schools have afternoon activities such as sports and crafts. Some children take music lessons at home. After school, they do their homework, play sports, or watch television. Since school is so important, they spend many hours studying.

Lucciola, Lucciola
(Firefly, Firefly)

This rhyme is from Tuscany, but it is known all over Italy. Children recite it while chasing fireflies on summer evenings.

Lucciola, lucciola, gialla, gialla
Metti la briglia alla cavalla
Che la vuole il figlio del re
Lucciola, lucciola, vieni con me.

Firefly, firefly, yellow and bright
Bridle the filly under your light
The son of the king is ready to ride
Firefly, firefly, fly by my side.

Just for Fun

Italians are big sports fans. In fact, Italy's best-selling newspaper is only about sports! They especially like soccer, which is called *il calcio*. Children start playing the game at a young age and never lose their love for it. On Sundays, Italians watch soccer games on TV or in the stands. They cheer for their favorite professional team playing in a large stadium. And they cheer just as hard for their local team playing on the village's soccer field.

Boys playing soccer

Skiers from all over the world come to Italy's slopes.

The Grand Tour of Italy, an annual event

Skiing, tennis, and biking are also popular. Il Giro d'Italia (Grand Tour of Italy) is an annual cycling event. For three weeks, men from around the world race each other all around the country. The hardest part of the course is through the mountain roads of the Alps. Every spring, Italians watch the race live on television.

Many Italians go bicycling for fun.

In addition to sports, Italians also have fun with their families. They play cards or bingo, take long walks, or go for bike rides together. Picnics are the perfect way for Italians to enjoy their two favorite things—family and food. In August, most businesses close. Families head for the mountains or crowd onto the beaches. They spend their vacations far away from the city.

Italian children play some of the same games as children from other countries. Young children enjoy make-believe. Older children jump rope and play hide-and-seek, basketball, and handball. When they play tag, they yell, *T'ho preso!* (I got you!)

Once a year, Italy has a special contest just for kids. The city of Bologna holds a singing contest called Lo Zecchino d'Oro (gold coin). Children from all over Italy enter. There is no prize, but the children have the chance to sing on television!

At home, Italian children like to collect stickers, shells, or rocks. Today, they also log

A boy prepares for a ball game at the beach.

Children at play in Venice

onto the Internet. They enjoy going to the movies, too. But in southern Italy, no popcorn for them! They can choose snacks like pizza, fried rice balls, and sausage. And they do more than just watch the movie. Italian children of all ages subscribe to the *cineforum*. Once a month, they see a movie in the theater, and afterward stay to discuss it.

Playing *Bocce*

As with many traditions in Italy, the game of *bocce* is very old. The ancient Greeks brought *bocce* with them when they settled in Italy. It is the ancestor of the game of bowling. Two to eight players can participate. Each player gets two balls to roll toward a small ball called the *pallino*. The player who gets his ball closest to the *pallino* wins. *Bocce* is more than a game. It is a chance to be with friends in the village square and enjoy a favorite Italian pastime, friendly arguing.

Let's Celebrate!

Festivals light up Italian cities and villages every season of the year. Most are religious, like Christmas and Easter. Since every town has a patron saint, villagers also celebrate their saint's special day.

Children hold up their nativity scenes for the Pope to bless.

Five Santas in a gondola

Christmas is a time for Italian families to celebrate the birth of Jesus. Each region celebrates a little differently. In the south of Italy, people gather for a large fish dinner on Christmas Eve. After, they attend Midnight Mass. The next day, northerners and southerners alike serve a big meal of pasta and turkey or capon. After Christmas dinner, families often play *tombola*, a game like bingo.

Families put up Christmas trees and nativity scenes, and children look forward to presents. Babbo Natale (Father Christmas) brings presents to children in some parts of Italy. In other regions, La Befana (The Good Witch) delivers stockings filled with gifts on the Epiphany, at the end of the Christmas season. And in still other areas, Saint Lucy brings treats to good children.

An Easter procession depicts Christ with his cross.

Easter celebrations begin the Wednesday before the holiday. In many villages, almost everyone will march in processions and act out scenes from the life of Jesus. On Easter Sunday, children receive gifts of chocolate eggs and lambs. In

A girl dressed for Carnevale feeds pigeons in Venice.

the province of Palermo, monks honor a three-hundred-year-old tradition. During the winter, they rescue birds from the cold and keep them in an aviary. On Easter Sunday, they set them free and celebrate the arrival of spring with a concert. Easter Monday is a national holiday, which families celebrate with huge picnics.

Italians love the processions, the music, and the pageantry of festivals. They take great pride in holding colorful events. Sometime between mid-January and February, for ten days before the start of Lent, Italians celebrate Carnevale. Wearing masks is an important part of the celebration. Both children and adults dress up in costumes and wear masks. Children even go to school in their costumes.

No city in Italy celebrates Carnevale more than Venice. Beginning with the Children's Carnival in Saint Mark's Square in the heart of the city, the celebration continues with concerts and masked balls. People stroll in costumes until the festival ends with fireworks in the square the night before Ash Wednesday.

Every harvest is another excuse to celebrate. The wine, grape, apple, and cherry festivals mean music, food, and contests. Even political debates are the basis for a three-week celebration. To the debates, Italians add concerts, art shows, dancing, and sports. In fact, Italians like to celebrate so much, the country has a festival for almost every day of the year!

A trumpeter at one of Italy's many festivals

Battle of the Oranges

During Carnevale, the town of Ivrea holds a Battle of the Oranges. This festival celebrates an uprising of the people against the ruling class in the twelfth century. Every *piazza* in the city is decorated. For three days, rival teams throw oranges at carts full of men who battle back. They use four hundred tons of oranges! A jury decides on the winning team, that is, the team that decorated their *piazza* best and had the best aim. Meanwhile, there are parades and pageants. The festivities end with a codfish feast.

The Italian flag is green, white, and red. It was first used in 1797.

Italy is a member of the European Union (EU). In January 2002, Italy and eleven other states within the EU began to use the same currency, or money. This currency is called the Euro. Euro coins share common European designs on the front, but the designs on the back of the coins change from nation to nation. Euro banknotes, or paper money, are the same in all twelve nations.

Count in Italian

English	Italian	Say it like this:
one	uno	OO-no
two	due	DEW-eh
three	tre	TREH
four	quattro	KWAT-tro
five	cinque	CHIN-kweh
six	sei	SAY
seven	sette	SET-teh
eight	otto	OH-toe
nine	nove	NO-veh
ten	dieci	dee-EH-chee

Glossary

aviary A place for keeping birds.

buon giorno (bwon-JOR-no) Good day.

calcio (CAL-cho) Soccer.

capon Type of chicken.

ciao (CHOW) Hello or good-bye.

cineforum Discussion group for children after they have seen a movie.

dormant Resting; describes a volcano that is not active.

Epiphany (eh-PIF-ah-nee) Feast of the Three Kings celebrated January 6th.

risotto (rih-SO-to) Rice dish from Northern Italy.

soprano People who sing or musical instruments whose sound is in the highest range.

Proud to Be Italian

Leonardo da Vinci (1452–1519)

The great Renaissance artist Leonardo da Vinci was born in 1452 outside of Vinci, a town near Florence. As a teenager, he was apprenticed to an artist from whom he learned to paint. As da Vinci grew older, he also became interested in science. On his own, he studied engineering, biology, mathematics, and physics. Many of his drawings show his interest in machines and how they work. Leonardo da Vinci is known for his life-sized painting *The Last Supper*. Copies of this great work are sold around the world, but the original is in a church in Milan. His portrait *Mona Lisa* is probably the most famous painting in the world.

Maria Montessori (1870–1952)

Although Maria Montessori was born more than one hundred years ago, she was a modern woman. At a time when women were only allowed to work as teachers, she wanted to be a doctor. She fought prejudice, and became Italy's first woman doctor. Montessori was especially interested in children. She studied the different ways they learn and combined this knowledge with her medical experience. She opened schools that helped children develop both intelligence and independence. Her fame spread, and Montessori schools were established throughout the world. She continued to travel, teach, and lecture until her death in 1952.

Alberto Tomba (1966–   )

When it comes to Olympic skiers, Alberto Tomba is known around the world. He is named among the Top Ten Winter Olympics athletes of all time. He was born in 1966, and, at the age of twenty-two, he won his first Olympic gold medal. He won gold again in the next Winter Olympics. It is not surprising that he is a favorite among sports fans. Tomba, known affectionately as La Bomba (The Bomb), is the skier who has won the most Olympic medals, five in all.

Find Out More

Books

Country Studies: Italy by Fred Martin. Heinemann Library, Illinois, 1999.

Look What Came from Italy by Miles Harvey. Franklin Watts, Connecticut, 1999.

The Buried City of Pompeii by Shelley Tanaka. Disney Press, New York, 1997.

Where We Live: Italy by Donna Bailey and Anna Sproule. Raintree Steck-Vaughn, Texas, 1990.

Web Sites

www.yahooligans.com/around_the_world/countries/Italy
Links to photographs and maps of Italy, plus numerous sites on the country's culture and history.

http://sunsite.berkeley.edu/KidsClick!
Type in *Italy* and this Web search will list half a dozen sites on travel, architecture, history, and geography.

Video

Rome & Pompeii, Global Video, Scottsdale, Arizona.
Computer-generated images of what these historic cities looked like.

Index

Page numbers for illustrations are in **boldface.**

About the Author

From the time she was a child, Margaret Gay Malone has loved books and reading. That interest turned into a love of writing. She has published four other books—three of them for children—and has written another book in this series, *France*. Two more of her children's books are due out this year. She likes to travel and counts Rome and Florence among her favorite cities. Margaret and her husband, Tom, have a daughter, Michele. They share their home in Sea Cliff, Long Island, with their dog and two cats.